nd mad !!.

How I love You

# In the Llama Yard

by Patricia M. Stockland
illustrated by Todd Ouren

Special thanks to content consultant:
James S. Cullor, DVM, PhD

**visit us at www.abdopublishing.com**

Published by Magic Wagon, a division of the ABDO Group, 8000 West 78th Street, Edina, Minnesota 55439. Copyright © 2010 by Abdo Consulting Group, Inc. International copyrights reserved in all countries. All rights reserved. No part of this book may be reproduced in any form without written permission from the publisher.

Looking Glass Library™ is a trademark and logo of Magic Wagon.

Printed in the United States.

Manufactured with paper containing at least 10% post-consumer waste

Text by Patricia M. Stockland
Illustrations by Todd Ouren
Edited by Amy Van Zee
Interior layout and design by Becky Daum
Cover design by Becky Daum

**Library of Congress Cataloging-in-Publication Data**
Stockland, Patricia M.
  In the llama yard / by Patricia M. Stockland ; illustrated by Todd Ouren.
      p. cm. — (Barnyard buddies)
  Includes index.
  ISBN 978-1-60270-644-6
  1. Llamas—Juvenile literature.  I. Ouren, Todd, ill. II. Title.
  SF401.L6S677 2010
  636.2'966—dc22

                              2009007481

The spring days are getting warmer. The sun shines on the llama yard. The female llama calls to her cria.

**Hum, hum, hmm . . .**

A cria is a baby llama.

The cria was born only an hour ago. But it is already strong enough to stand. The cria calls back to its mother. **Hmm . . . hum . . .**

Llamas make low, humming sounds to each other.
Llamas can make other sounds to "speak" too.

5

The hungry cria drinks milk from its mother. The milk is full of nutrients. It helps the young cria grow big and strong.

Llamas weigh between 20 and 30 pounds at birth. They are covered in soft wool.

Soon, it is time to join the herd. The other llamas are grazing in the yard.

A group of llamas is called a herd.

As the cria gets older, it learns to eat solid foods. The farmer feeds the herd bales of hay. The llamas also eat grass.

A llama's stomach has three parts. These separate parts help it digest rough foods.

When the cria is about six months old, it no longer needs milk. The farmer weans the cria from its mother.

Weaning is when the cria is
separated from its mother.

The weaned llama will learn many jobs.
Some adult llamas protect other animals
from predators.

Some farms use llamas to protect
smaller animals, such as sheep.

As autumn nears, the llamas help the farmer pull small carts. Llamas can also carry packs for people.

Llamas are smart. They can be trained
to help people do lots of jobs.

Springtime arrives again. The adult llamas'
wool has become thick. It is shearing time
for the herd.

Llamas are usually sheared each year in the spring. Their wool is used for clothing, rugs, and other woven items.

19

Next spring, the young llama will also be sheared. For now, it is busy learning to help on the farm. The llamas call to each other in the yard. **Hum, hum, hmm . . .**

21

# Llama Diagram

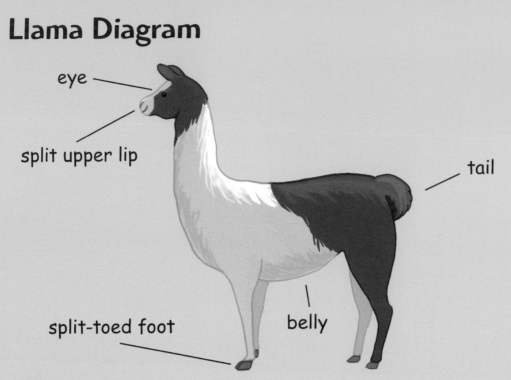

eye

split upper lip

tail

split-toed foot

belly

# Glossary

**digest**—to break down food into pieces small enough for the body to take in.

**graze**—to feed on land covered by grass.

**nutrients**—vitamins and other things in food that are good for growth and health.

**predator**—an animal that hunts other animals.

# Fun Facts

 Around 1900, people started bringing llamas to the United States from other countries.

 Llamas were originally domesticated, or trained to help people, in South America.

 Llamas are very social animals. They like to be part of a herd.

 To show who is boss, llamas will spit at each other.

 Llamas are very smart and very curious. They are also naturally calm and quiet.

 Llamas can work as companion pets. They can even be trained to carry golf clubs!

 Because of their sure footing and smarts, llamas make great pack animals on hiking trails.

 Llamas can live to be more than 25 years old.

# Index